This book belongs to:

_____

THANK YOU FOR YOUR PURCHASE!

The Dream Catcher Coloring Book by Vendetta Color Expressions is an Native American dream catcher themed coloring book for teens and adults. Our goal at Vendetta Color Expressions is to create high quality, unique coloring books by combining the works of several amazing artists to capture the essence of the book's theme. We are always working to come up with interesting ideas for new art books, so please check out our full collection on Amazon.com and consider leaving us some honest feedback.

Thank you supporting woman-owned small businesses.

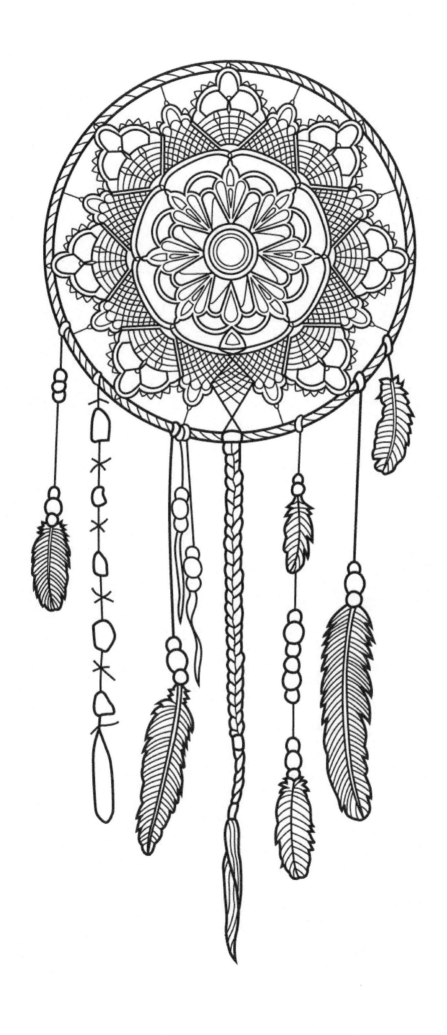

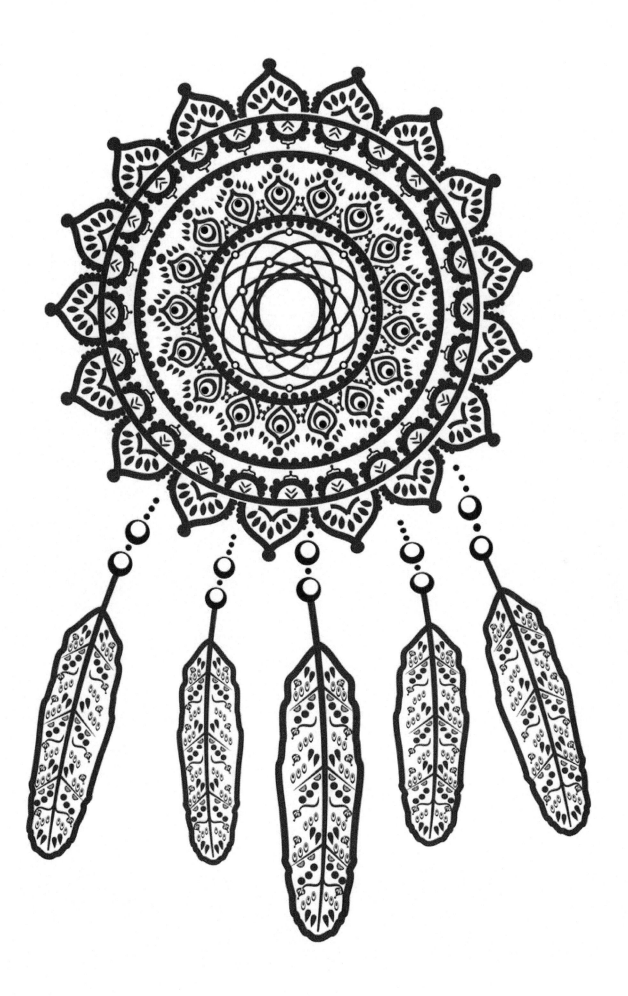

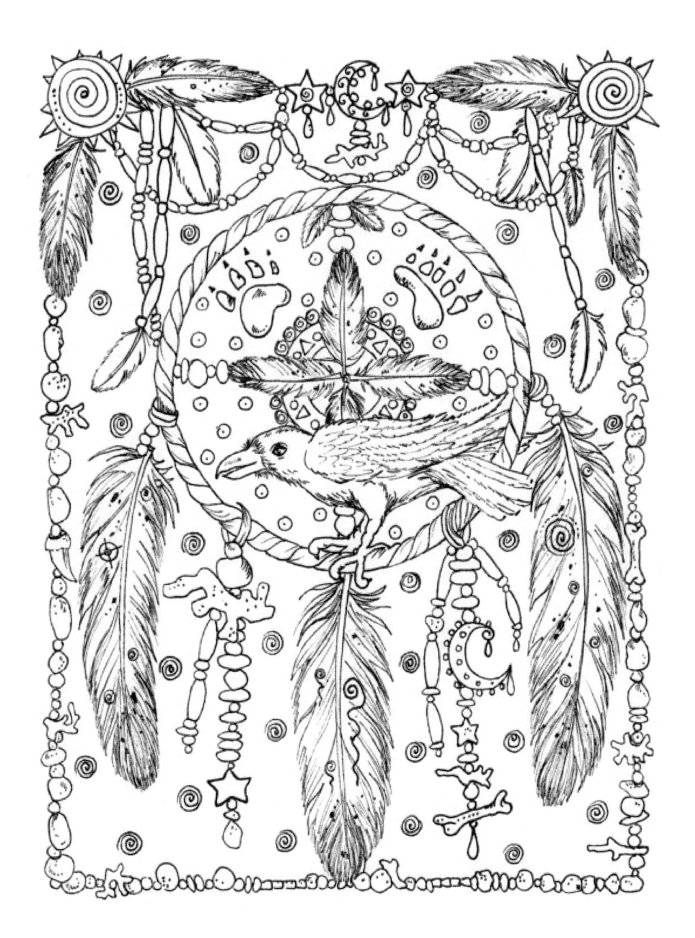

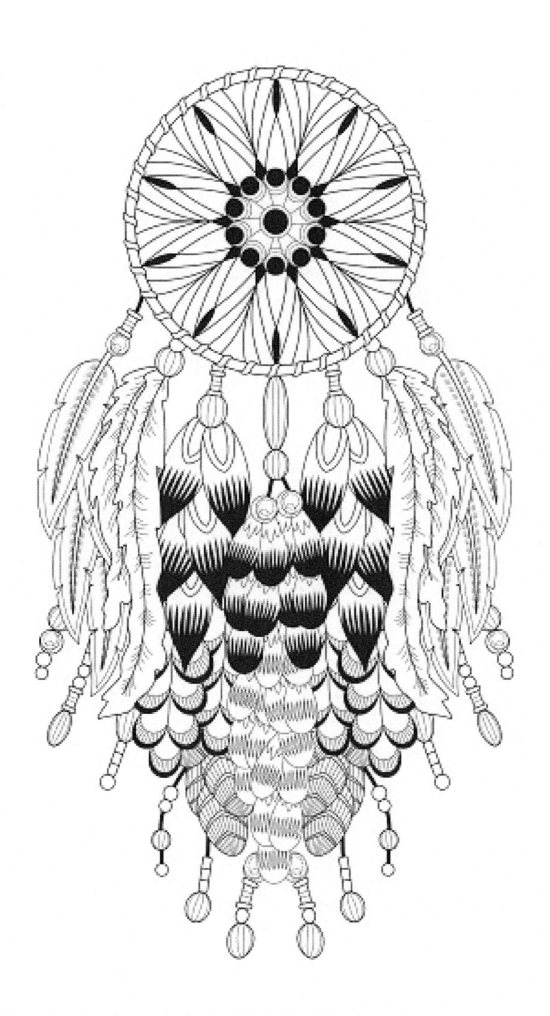

MORE FROM VENDETTA COLOR EXPRESSIONS

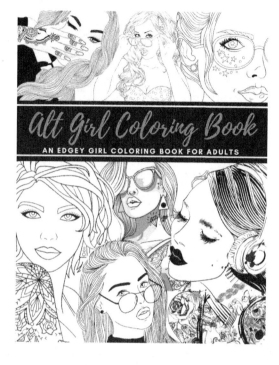

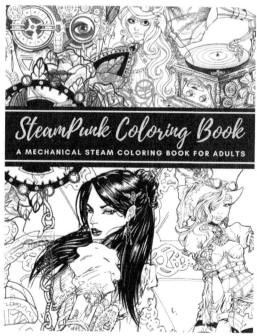

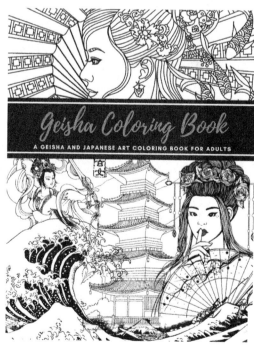

BY VENDETTA

FOLLOW ME ON SOCIAL MEDIA!

   @VendettaColorEx

   @VendettaColorEx

   /@VendettaColorEx

Printed in Great Britain
by Amazon

17316046R00086